BRITISH RAILWAYS STEAMING FROM 1948–1968

Compiled by
PETER HANDS

DEFIANT PUBLICATIONS
190 Yoxall Road,
Shirley, Solihull,
West Midlands

Printed on behalf of Richard Netherwood Limited, by Gorenjski tisk p.o. Slovenia.

CURRENT STEAM PHOTOGRAPH ALBUMS AVAILABLE
FROM DEFIANT PUBLICATIONS

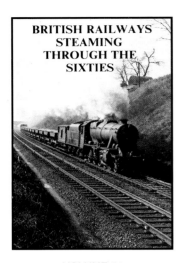

VOLUME 14
A4 size - Hardback. 96 pages
-178 b/w photographs.
£14.95 + £1.50 postage.
ISBN 0 946857 40 7.

VOLUME 15
A4 size - Hardback. 96 pages
-178 b/w photographs.
£16.95 + £1.50 postage.
ISBN 0 946857 52 0.

BRITISH RAILWAYS
STEAMING
THROUGH THE
SIXTIES

IN
PREPARATION

VOLUME 16

VOLUME 1
A4 size - Hardback. 96 pages
-177 b/w photographs.
£14.95 + £1.50 postage.
ISBN 0 946857 41 5.

VOLUME 9
A4 size - Hardback. 96 pages
-177 b/w photographs.
£14.95 + £1.50 postage.
ISBN 0 946857 37 7.

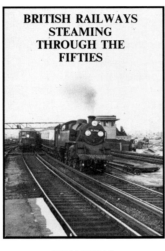

VOLUME 10
A4 size - Hardback. 96 pages
-176 b/w photographs.
£14.95 + £1.50 postage.
ISBN 0 946857 38 5.

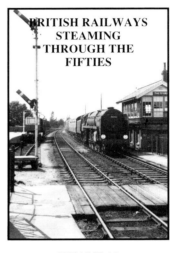

VOLUME 11
A4 size - Hardback. 96 pages
-176 b/w photographs.
£16.95 + £1.50 postage.
ISBN 0 946857 48 2.

VOLUME 12
A4 size - Hardback. 96 pages
-176 b/w photographs.
£16.95 + £1.50 postage.
ISBN 0 946857 49 0.

VOLUME 1
A4 size - Hardback. 96 pages
-177 b/w photographs.
£14.95 + £1.50 postage.
ISBN 0 946857 39 3.

VOLUME 1
A4 size - Hardback. 96 pages
-174 b/w photographs.
£14.95 + £1.50 postage.
ISBN 0 946857 42 3.

VOLUME 1
A4 size - Hardback. 96 pages
-179 b/w photographs.
£15.95 + £1.50 postage.
ISBN 0 946857 43 I.

VOLUME 3
A4 size - Hardback. 96 pages
-183 b/w photographs.
£15.95 + £1.50 postage.
ISBN 0 946857 44 X.

FUTURE STEAM PHOTOGRAPH ALBUMS
AND OTHER TITLES

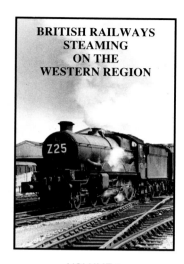

**BRITISH RAILWAYS
STEAMING
ON THE
WESTERN REGION**

VOLUME 4
A4 size - Hardback. 96 pages
-177 b/w photographs.
£15.95 + £1.50 postage.
ISBN 0 946857 46 6.

**EARLY AND PIONEER
DIESEL & ELECTRIC
LOCOMOTIVES
OF BRITISH RAILWAYS**

A4 size - Hardback. 96 pages
-177 b/w photographs.
£15.95 + £1.50 postage.
ISBN 0 946857 45 8.

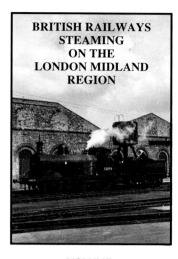

**BRITISH RAILWAYS
STEAMING
ON THE
LONDON MIDLAND
REGION**

VOLUME 4
A4 size - Hardback. 96 pages
-177 b/w photographs.
£15.95 + £1.50 postage.
ISBN 0 946857 47 4.

**BRITISH RAILWAYS
STEAMING
ON THE
SOUTHERN REGION**

**IN
PREPARATION**

VOLUME 3

**BRITISH RAILWAYS
STEAM HAULED
TITLED TRAINS**

A4 size - Hardback. 96 pages
-169 b/w photographs.
£16.95 + £1.50 postage.
ISBN 0 946857 51 2.

**BRITISH RAILWAYS
STEAMING
THROUGH CREWE,
DONCASTER,
EASTLEIGH AND
SWINDON**

**IN
PREPARATION**

**BRITISH RAILWAYS
STEAMING
THROUGH LONDON**

**IN
PREPARATION**

**BRITISH RAILWAYS
STEAMING ON
THE EX-LNER
LINES**

**IN
PREPARATION**

VOLUME 4

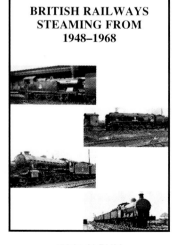

**BRITISH RAILWAYS
STEAMING FROM
1948–1968**

'50th' ALBUM
A4 size - Hardback. 96 pages
-186 b/w photographs.
£16.95 + £1.50 postage.
ISBN 0 946857 50 4.

**BRITISH RAILWAYS
STEAM HAULED
PASSENGER TRAINS
IN THE
FIFTIES**

**IN
PREPARATION**

VOLUME 2

**BRITISH RAILWAYS
STEAM HAULED
PASSENGER TRAINS
IN THE
SIXTIES**

**IN
PREPARATION**

VOLUME 2

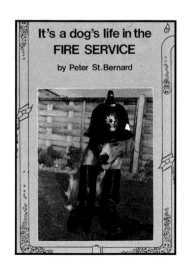

It's a dog's life in the
FIRE SERVICE
by Peter St. Bernard

COMEDY
269 pages. Cartoons.
£9.95 + £1.00 postage.
ISBN 0 946857 30 X.

ACKNOWLEDGEMENTS

Grateful thanks are extended to the following contributors of photographs not only for their use in this book but for their kind patience and long term loan of negatives/ photographs whilst this book was being compiled.

R.BUTTERFIELD MIRFIELD	R.S.CARPENTER BIRMINGHAM	S.DARTNELL DERBY
TIM FAREBROTHER BOURTON	J.M.GASCOYNE HIGH WYCOMBE	A.N.H.GLOVER BIRMINGHAM
J.D.GOMERSALL SHEFFIELD	B.K.B.GREEN WARRINGTON	PETER HAY HOVE
JOHN HEAD EASTBOURNE	R.W.HINTON GLOUCESTER	H.L.HOLLAND ST.CATHERINES, ONTARIO, CANADA
F.HORNBY NORTH CHEAM	JOHN HOSSACK UNKNOWN	A.C.INGRAM WISBECH
R.G.B.JACKSON KEMPSTON	D.K.JONES MOUNTAIN ASH	M.JOYCE HITCHIN
T.LEWIS *	A.F.NISBET BRACKLEY	T.B.OWEN CAEMELYN
R.PICTON WOLVERHAMPTON	W.G.PIGGOTT UNKNOWN	A.J.PIKE **
N.E.PREEDY HUCCLECOTE	J.H.PRICE ***	GEOFF READMAN UNKNOWN
P.A.ROWLINGS ALCONBURY	J.SCHATZ LITTLETHORPE	K.L.SEAL ANDOVERSFORD
C.P.STACEY STONY STRATFORD	M.S.STOKES MARPLE	D.TITHERIDGE FAREHAM
M.TURNER BROAD HINTON	D.WEBSTER *	KIT WINDLE LOWER BREDBURY
MIKE WOOD BIRMINGHAM		

*	Courtesy of the Norman Preedy collection
**	Courtesy of the Frank Hornby collection
***	Courtesy of the Andrew Ingram collection

Front Cover - upper left:- GWR 5600 Class 0-6-2T No 6650, from 87A Neath, stands in Cardiff (General) station with the stock of a passenger train on 11th April 1955. (R.W.Hinton) Front Cover - upper right:- SR Rebuilt *Battle of Britain* Class 4-6-2 No 34050 *Royal Observer Corps* stands in the yard of its home shed at 70A Nine Elms on 1st May 1964. (A.C.Ingram) Front Cover - lower left:- LNER B1 Class 4-6-0 No 61250 *A.Harold Bibby*, of 36A Doncaster, is a visitor to 52A Gateshead in October 1956 from 36A Doncaster. (R.W.Hinton) Front Cover - lower right:- LNWR Class 7F 0-8-0 No 49150 (10B Preston) plods along at Farington with a short train of empties on 4th May 1957. (R.W.Hinton)

ISBN 0 946857 50 4

© P.B.HANDS 1995
FIRST PUBLISHED

INTRODUCTION

BRITISH RAILWAYS STEAMING FROM 1948-1968 is a 'one-off' special album designed to acknowledge a milestone for 'Defiant Publications' in the fact that this is the '50th' railway photograph album to be published.

When the first album, 'BR STEAMING THROUGH THE SIXTIES - Volume One', appeared in print during 1983 the thought never occurred to the author that the albums would still be going strong twelve years later.

The author would like to take this opportunity to thank each and every customer who has enjoyed these books over the years. I would also like to thank the many contributors of photographs, for without their photographs these books would not exist. I would also like to extend a special 'thank you' to Roger Carpenter and Frank Hornby for their help in compiling some of the captions for this album.

BR STEAMING FROM 1948-1968 takes us on a journey from the inception of British Railways through to the end of steam and covers many locations throughout the length and breadth of our island. Bearing in mind that this album celebrates a 'Golden Anniversary' there are many prints included of locomotives ending with the prefix '50'.

The author hopes the reader will enjoy the diverse variety of locations and locomotives within the pages of this album. the 'BR Steaming' books are designed to give the ordinary, everyday steam photographic enthusiast of the 1950's and 1960's a chance to participate in and give pleasure to others whilst recapturing the twilight days of steam.

Apart from the 1950's and 1960's series, individual albums will be produced from time to time. Wherever possible no famous names will be used, nor will photographs which have been published before be used, but the content and quality of the majority of photographs used will be second to none.

As a footnote, the author would like to point out that somewhere near a total of 9000 photographs have been published in these albums to date.

'Defiant Publications' is only a small organisation and rarely receives any publicity. The continuation of the photograph albums depends upon *you* the reader. Who knows, one day the 'Centenary' of albums might appear in print? If you wish to join my mailing list for future albums and/or feel you have suitable material of BR steam locomotives between 1948-1968 and wish to contribute them towards future albums, please contact:-

Tel. No.
0121 745-8421

Peter Hands,
190 Yoxall Road,
Shirley, Solihull,
West Midlands B90 3RN

CONTENTS

1) We begin this special '50th' commemorative album on a sad note with two locomotives which have been involved in accidents. Observers and railwaymen alike are gathered near to the lifeless form of LNER A2/1 Class 4-6-2 No 60508 *Duke of Rothesay* as it ignominiously lies on its side stripped of coal supplies at New Southgate on 17th July 1948 awaiting the breakdown trains which will right it, before transportation to Doncaster Works. (B.W.L.Brooksbank)

2) The damage to LMS *Coronation* Class 4-6-2 No 6251 *City of Nottingham*, from 12B Carlisle (Upperby), is plain for all to see as it stands in the yard at Crewe Works on 17th April 1948 in the company of LMS Class 4 2-6-4T No 2663. *City of Nottingham* had been involved in a bad collision at Winsford whilst hauling the southbound *West Coast Postal* at midnight on 16th April 1948 with the 5.40pm Glasgow to Euston which was stationary at the time. (B.W.L.Brooksbank)

3) Newly adorned with a fresh coat of lined livery LMS Class 5 4-6-0 No 4763 stands in the yard of its home shed at 5A Crewe (North) on 7th March 1948 with the stencilled markings of its new owner on the tender. Note the letters 'M' above the cabside number and also alongside the smokebox numberplate. No (4)4763 remained at Crewe North depot for many years before moving on to 1G Woodford Halse and 1A Willesden during 1965. (A.N.H.Glover)

4) A brand new Southern Railway inspired Unrebuilt *Battle of Britain* Class 4-6-2 No 34082 *615 Squadron* emerges from Chislehurst tunnel near Elmstead Woods station on the former South Eastern and Chatham Railway main line out of London to the Kent Coast via Hither Green and Orpington Junction in September 1948. Between the late fifties and withdrawal in April 1966, No 34082 worked at a variety of sheds. It was rebuilt in April 1960 at Eastleigh. (D.K.Jones)

5) Ex. GCR 0-6-2T No E9349 (LNER N5 Class) stands outside the Great Central shed at Wrexham on 25th July 1948. This depot, known as Wrexham (Rhosddu) after 1948, was originally that of the Wrexham, Mold and Connahs Quay Railway which was absorbed by the GCR in 1905. The loco carries the early style of BR livery of 'British Railways' in full with the short-lived temporary suffix applied to some engines from the 'Big Four', in this case 'E' for LNER groups. (A.N.H.Glover)

6) LMS Fowler Class 4 2-6-4T No 2412 basks in the sun outside the former London and North Western Railway shed at Huddersfield on 2nd May 1948 still carrying its LMS livery. It was not until about 1950 that the British Railways corporate livery was generally applied to the lesser prestigious locomotive classes. No (4)2412 remained at Huddersfield shed until withdrawn from service in January 1962. It was scrapped at Derby Works the same month. (A.N.H.Glover)

7) Another example of a locomotive sporting the logos and livery of its former owner, the London and North Eastern Railway, is B1 Class 4-6-0 No 1277 which is in post-war apple green. This locomotive would have still been relatively new when photographed outside the ex. Great North of Scotland Railway shed at Kittybrewster on 7th June 1948. During the latter years of its life No (6)1277 served at 65A Eastfield, 62A Thornton Junction and 62B Dundee. (W.G.Boyden)

8) Amongst some of the oddities inherited from the 'Big Four' was this example of a crane tank which owed its parentage to the SECR. 1302 Class 0-4-0CT No 1302 is seen at Stewarts Lane (Battersea) shed on 29th August 1948. Built by Neilson & Co. in 1881 it was numbered A2345 until 1938. It was used to shunt the CWS milk depot until taken out of traffic in July 1949. As far as is known it carried its SR livery until the end and was never renumbered in BR stock. (T.B.Owen)

9) With the wheels of industry smoking in the background former North British Railway N15 Class 0-6-0T No 9148 ambles along on quadruped track at Craigentinny on the outskirts of Edinburgh with a lengthy pick-up freight on 16th August 1948. No 9148 was probably based at the large complex of St.Margarets shed. Withdrawn in June 1958, No (6) 9148 was stored at 64E Polmont and 64F Bathgate until despatched to Kilmarnock for scrapping in early 1959. (B.W.L.Brooksbank)

10) During 1948 the newly formed Railway Executive carried out various locomotive exchange trials utilising engines from the 'Big Four' on other parts of the system to help assess locomotive development/performance for the future BR Standard classes of the 1950's. Here we see LMS Class 5 4-6-0 No 45253 in the early BR livery pulling away from Dawlish Warren station with the 1.45pm express from Bristol to Plymouth on 3rd July 1948. (D.K.Jones)

11) Here is a 'Sassenach' well north of the border in the unlikely shape of ex. GER F4 Class 2-4-2T No 7157 which is posing between shunting operations at Inverurie Works on 8th June 1949. There were in fact a trio of these locomotives stationed at Kittybrewster (Aberdeen) shed in early BR days and this particular example, with a short stovepipe chimney, remained there until June 1956, being the last working representative of the class. (A.N.H.Glover)

12) Another example of early BR livery is seen in this photograph of SR H15 Class 4-6-0 No 30522 seen at Eastleigh shed on 11th June 1949. This engine, built by the SR in 1924 after grouping, still carries the SR paintwork, but with a BR number. A lot of locomotives were so treated during 1948 to save a full repaint. Sometimes this treatment was undertaken at the larger depots where there were adjoining workshops facilities. (B.K.B.Green)

13) An impressive close-up of GWR/ROD Class 2-8-0 No 3032 as it stands at rest over an ashpit within the confines of a roundhouse at St.Philip's Marsh shed in Bristol on 19th June 1949. No 3032 is almost certainly in GWR livery, but with the addition of a British Railways front numberplate on the smokebox. This was a common practise during the 1948-1950 period. By January 1957 only six GWR examples were still at work but they were gone by late 1958. (R.S.Carpenter)

14) Steam escaping from the safety valves of ex. GCR D9 Class 4-4-0 No 62333 obscures the signalbox at Cheadle station as it arrives tender-first under clear signals with a six coach local passenger train on 11th September 1949. Evening shadows fall as the train of former Great Central Railway compartment stock heads eastwards from Warrington (Central) to Stockport (Tiviot Dale). The Class was rendered extinct well before the fifties ended. (R.W.Hinton)

15) Another photograph of Elmstead Woods, this time from the station itself as December 1948 constructed Unrebuilt *Battle of Britain* Class 4-6-2 No 34086 rushes through with Kent Coast express on 12th April 1949. No 34086, later named *219 Squadron*, is again in early BR Southern livery. During the latter stages of its career, No 34086 was based at 74B Ramsgate, 72A Exmouth Junction (twice), 74C Dover, 73A Stewarts Lane and 70D Eastleigh. (D.K.Jones)

16) On a bright summer's day former NBR C16 Class 4-4-2T No 67493 stands outside the entrance to the shed at 62B Dundee Tay Bridge on 8th June 1949. Note the livery style of No 67493. In the early days of BR there was a tendency to experiment with lining on tank engines. Usually the lining followed the contours of the tanks, but in this case a somewhat unusual style has been adopted here. Three members of this class survived until April 1961. (A.N.H.Glover)

17) The locomotive depot at Carstairs, once owned by the Caledonian Railway, came under the LMR from 1948-49, coded 28C. After 1949 it belonged to the Scottish Region, carrying the codes of 64D and 66E until closure in December 1966. On 9th June 1949, one of its residents, LMS Class 4 2-6-4T No 42173, shows off it's gleaming paintwork. Note the 'star' on the smokebox door. A longstanding inmate of Carstairs, No 42173 was withdrawn in December 1962. (A.N.H.Glover)

18) The oval combined name and numberplates on the cabside of GWR 'Bulldog' 3300 Class 4-4-0 No 3341 *Blasius* is clearly visible in this excellent study at Exeter (St.Davids) station on 5th June 1949 where it is in charge of a local passenger. *Blasius* was one of 41 engines to carry this style of nameplate and was the first of the class with straight frames. Although looking in fine external condition withdrawal was only five months away. (B.K.B.Green)

19) Bright sunshine reflects off the exterior of LMS Fowler Class 3 2-6-2T No 40006, a local engine, as it stands in the shed yard at 1A Willesden in the company of former Midland Railway Class 2F 0-6-0 No 58303 in the summer of 1950. No 40006 remained loyal to Willesden shed until January 1959 when it was drafted to Wolverton Works. It returned to Willesden in May 1961 but was withdrawn in October 1962 after spending several months in store. (B.K.B.Green)

20) A heavy duty former Great Central Railway A5 Class 4-6-2 No 69807 sizzles virtually unnoticed by the railway passengers as it waits in a bay platform at Rickmansworth station on the GCR/MET line to take over a Metropolitan train to Aylesbury in July 1950. Although by January 1957 the class of thirty engines were still intact, the writing was on the wall for these engines and they were all gone by November 1960. (D.K.Jones)

21) Although a front numberplate has been fitted GWR *Hall* Class 4-6-0 No 4923 *Evenley Hall* is still in post-war livery and sporting GWR on its tender as it approaches Shrewsbury station at Crewe Junction with an express from Chester in October 1950. During the late fifties *Evenley Hall* was based at 87E Landore, but during 1960 there was a flurry of activity as it moved to 84C Banbury, 87G Carmarthen and 84A Wolverhampton (Stafford Road). (D.K.Jones)

22) This scene taken in the shed yard at 66A Polmadie (Glasgow) in March 1950 offers a nice contrast between an ex. Caledonian Railway Class 3F 0-6-0T No 56306 and one of its LMS built 'Jinty' successor's whose identity is obscured by a member of the footplate staff. At this date in time there were twenty of the Caledonian 3F's and six 'Jinties' on the books at Polmadie. No 56306 survived in service at the depot until December 1958. (D.K.Jones)

23) The Great Eastern meets the Great Northern on the former's metals at 30A Stratford in London on 30th April 1950. Centrepiece of this study is GNR J50 Class 0-6-0T No 68950 in the company of GER N7 Class 0-6-2T No 69703 which was withdrawn from 30A in January 1959 and scrapped at the nearby workshops. No 68950 served from 38A/40E Colwick, 34B Hornsey and 34A Kings Cross before succumbing to the inevitable fate in September 1961. (R.W.Hinton)

24) A feather of steam escapes from the safety valves of LMS Rebuilt *Patriot* Class 4-6-0 No 45540 *Sir Robert Turnbull* as it awaits departure from Shrewsbury station with a south-west to north-west express in April 1950. Later equipped with large smoke deflectors, *Sir Robert Turnbull* was allocated to 9A Longsight (Manchester), 3B/21C Bushbury, 9E Trafford Park, 21A Saltley, 17A Derby and 12B Carlisle (Upperby) before being condemned in April 1963. (D.K.Jones)

25) Steam seeps from the cylinders of SR *King Arthur* Class 4-6-0 No 30773 *Sir Lavaine* (70A Nine Elms) as it departs from Waterloo station with the 10.54am semi-fast passenger train bound for Bournemouth on 24th June 1950. During its latter days of revenue earning service, *Sir Lavaine* was based at 71B Bournemouth, 70D Basingstoke and 71A Eastleigh. It was withdrawn from the latter in February 1962 and cut up at Eastleigh Works two months later. (B.W.L.Brooksbank)

26) A thoroughly 'Westernised' Riches Taff Vale Railway O4 Class 0-6-2T No 67 (Manning-Wardle 1701/1907) as GWR No 294 on Swindon Works dump on 29th October 1950, following withdrawal. Rebuilt in 1929 at Caerphilly Works with a standard S3 boiler, the original TVR roundtopped side tanks were retained. These locomotives were used on mixed traffic duties from Cathays shed, Cardiff but were more widely dispersed following the 1923 grouping. (A.N.H.Glover)

27) A splendid view of part of the motive power depot, carriage shed and station at Ramsgate on 24th May 1951. The immediate scene is all but deserted except for the presence of SR L1 Class 4-4-0 No 31784, from 73B Bricklayers Arms, which is assembling some coaching stock. As electrification spread to the Kent Coast lines during the fifties, sheds like the one at Ramsgate soon closed to steam. No 31784 survived until February 1960. (B.K.B.Green)

28) Two outshopped locomotives await firing and returning to their home sheds in the yard at Horwich Works on 7th October 1951. Nearest the camera is 7A Llandudno Junction based LMS Class 3 2-6-2T No 40083 which later transferred to 3A Bescot from June 1958 to February 1962 before returning for a final spell at Llandudno prior to withdrawal in November 1962. Behind No 40083 is LMS Class 4F 0-6-0 No 44339, allocated to 9D Buxton. (B.K.B.Green)

29) By 1951 the first batch of BR *Britannia* Class 4-6-2's had come off the drawing board and emerged into revenue earning service on British Railways. No 70015 *Apollo* shows off its handsome lines in the shed yard at 8A Liverpool (Edge Hill) on 18th September 1961. For a while *Apollo* was one of a batch based at 86C Cardiff (Canton). It moved to the London Midland Region in July 1958 and served from numerous depots until it demise in August 1967. (A.N.H.Glover)

30) A fireman adopts a comfortable stance on the footplate of his charge, GWR 4300 Class 2-6-0 No 7308, as it waits in Shrewsbury station on 15th April 1951 to take over a local passenger service. The 7300 sequence of 2-6-0's eventually numbered forty-two units, although Nos 7322-41 were inherited from the earlier numbers 9300-19. No 7308 was based at a large number of depots on the Western Region until withdrawal in June 1964. (D.K.Jones)

31) Newly constructed and one of only three similar engines ever based on the Southern Region, BR *Britannia* Class 4-6-2 No 70009 *Alfred the Great* is ready to depart from Bournemouth (Central) with an up express bound for Waterloo on 19th July 1951. By January 1957 it was allocated to 32A Norwich where it remained until September 1961. Later transfers took *Alfred the Great* to 31B March and 12A Carlisle (Kingmoor) before withdrawal in January 1967. (D.K.Jones)

32) As previously mentioned in an earlier caption Wrexham shed was an outpost of the Great Central Railway. In British Railways days it came under the control of the London Midland Region from 1948-58, coded 6E, and finally under the Western Region from 1958 to closure on 23rd April 1960 as 84K. On 23rd July 1951, ex. GCR J62 Class 0-6-0ST No 68200, a Gorton Works product of 1897, is seen in the yard, just three months short of withdrawal. (N.E.Preedy)

33) LMS Unrebuilt *Royal Scot* Class 4-6-0 No 46148 *The Manchester Regiment*, from 1B Camden, takes a well earned rest in front of the shed building at 5A Crewe (North) on a murky and cold 25th November 1951. Later rebuilt with a taper boiler, double chimney and smoke deflectors, *The Manchester Regiment* also worked from 5A Crewe (North), 12A Carlisle (Upperby), 41C Millhouses, 1A Willesden and 6J Holyhead to mention but a few. (A.N.H.Glover)

34) When photographed light engine at Worcester (Shrub Hill) station on 24th July 1951, GWR *Saint* Class 4-6-0 No 2944 *Highnam Court* was not too far from its namesake, a stately home near Gloucester. *Highnam Court* was one of a batch of six such locomotives to emerge from Swindon Works in May 1912. It was rendered surplus to operating requirements on the Western Region in November 1951 and was presumably cut up at its birthplace. (N.E.Preedy)

35) Judging by the external appearance of SR O1 Class 0-6-0 No 31048 the cleaners at 74A Ashford have been at work. No 31048 is noted in the depot yard in the company of SR N Class 2-6-0 No 31402, a local inhabitant of Ashford on 4th October 1952. If on foot it was a good twenty-five minute walk to the shed from the local station. No 31048 was ousted from Ashford by modern traction in June 1959 and drafted away to London at 70A Nine Elms. (B.K.B.Green)

36) LNER B16/1 Class 5MT 4-6-0 No 61450, from 50A York, races south through Selby station with a fitted freight on 27th August 1952, passing some vintage carriages forming a Selby to Goole local train waiting to leave the up side bay platform. The handsome B16 Class engines were the last examples of Raven designed passenger locomotives to survive into the latter days of steam and were employed in the main on freight duties. (Peter Hay)

37) Sun, sea and sand on the South Devon coast at Dawlish on 28th August 1952. A Paddington to Plymouth express packed with excited holidaymakers approaches the camera hauled by a 'double-header'. In charge of the express is GWR *King* Class 4-6-0 No 6027 *King Richard I*, from 83D Laira (Plymouth), which is being piloted by GWR *Grange* Class 4-6-0 No 6822 *Manton Grange*, of 83A Newton Abbot, which ended its days at 82E Bristol Barrow Road. (D.K.Jones)

38) A long line-up of locomotives bask in warm spring sunshine in the yard at 9F Heaton Mersey on 13th April 1952. Leading the cavalcade is a smartly turned out LMS Class 2P 4-4-0 No 40693 which is a visitor to the depot from 9A Longsight (Manchester). This engine remained faithful to Longsight until no longer required in July 1959. After withdrawal it lay rotting and unwanted at Chaddesdon, Derby until September 1961 when it was cut up at Looms, Spondon. (B.K.B.Green)

39) From the spotless appearance of ex. Burry Port & Gwendraeth Valley Railway 0-6-0ST No 2176, seen resting in the shed yard at 88C Barry on 27th July 1952, it is obviously fresh from overhaul and on its way back to 87F Llanelly. On an adjacent road is the bulky shape of Hawksworth GWR 9400 Class 0-6-0PT No 8465, a local resident of 88C which was based later at 82C Swindon and 81A Old Oak Common before being taken out of traffic in November 1963. (B.K.B.Green)

40) No 55359 was the last surviving example of the twelve LMS Class 4P 4-6-2 Tanks constructed by the Caledonian Railway at St.Rollox Works during 1917. These locomotives were primarily designed for the Clyde coast suburban traffic, but most of them ended their days at Beattock on banking duties up the formidable incline. No 55359 assists a freight train out of Beattock station on 27th June 1952 a year or so before being withdrawn from service. (R.Butterfield)

41) The Edwardian locomotive engineers took great pride in producing machines which were elegant as well as efficient - none more so than Harry Wainwright of the South Eastern and Chatham Railway, designer of the fifty-one D Class 4-4-0's of which No 31577 is a member. A shunter hitches a free ride as No 31577 poses beneath an impressive signal gantry at Ashford station on 4th October 1952 as it waits to run light engine to the nearby shed. (B.K.B.Green)

42) The B2/B17 Classes of 4-6-0's and the B1 Class 4-6-0's were the mainstay of passenger workings to and from Liverpool Street station until the introduction of the vastly superior BR *Britannia* Class 4-6-2's in the early fifties. Known as the 'Sandringham' Class the B2/B17's were named after stately homes and famous football clubs. On 4th May 1952, No 61630 *Tottenham Hotspur* (withdrawn in September 1958) is seen at 31C Kings Lynn. (A.N.H.Glover)

65) Beyer-Garratt 2-8-0 + 0-8-2 No 69999 was a 'one-off' locomotive, built as U1 Class No 2395 in 1925 for banking duties on the 1 in 40 Worsborough incline between Wentworth Junction and Silkstone. Towards the end of its career it had a brief spell on the Lickey incline before going into store at Doncaster where we see it on 20th November 1955 shortly before withdrawal. With a tractive effort of 72,940 lbs. it was Britain's most powerful locomotive. (R.Butterfield)

66) The K Class 2-6-0's were first introduced into service by Billinton for the London, Brighton and South Coast Railway in 1913 and all in all a total of seventeen were constructed. They were later modified by Maunsell with lower domes and chimneys and standard cabs for better route availability. On 4th August No 32342 (75A Brighton) arrives at Redhill station with a mixed bag of stock. Note the ambulance vehicle protruding into the left of the frame. (B.K.B.Green)

67) The BR *Clan* Class 4-6-2's were the 'poor relations' in comparison with the powerful and popular *Britannia* Pacifics. First introduced into service during 1952 all were gone by May 1966 with the withdrawal of No 72006 *Clan Mackenzie*. Photographed at 68A Carlisle (Kingmoor) on 24th June 1956 is No 72004 *Clan MacDonald*, from 66A Polmadie (Glasgow), which was withdrawn in December 1962 from 66A and cut up at Darlington Works by March 1964. (J.D.Gomersall)

68) This view, looking west, shows the small terminus section of St.Erth station, built to serve the St.Ives branch in Cornwall. Out of sight in the left of the picture are the main line platforms. On 21st August 1956 a few passengers mill around the terminus as GWR 4500 Class 2-6-2T No 4574, from 83G Penzance fusses about with a single van. Constructed at Swindon Works in 1924, No 4574 remained in revenue earning service until February 1963. (N.L.Browne)

69) When sighted passing Ford station in Sussex in May 1956, SR A1X Class 0-6-0T No 32650 was en route from Littlehampton Wharf to 71D Fratton, the shed which also provided motive power for the Hayling Island branch. No 32650 has the extended bunker fitted for service on the Isle of Wight, a large toolbox dating from the 1946 oil firing trials, and a spark arrester on the chimney. Today, it is preserved on the Kent & East Sussex Railway. (Peter Hay)

70) Former Midland Railway 0-10-0 No 58100, affectionately known as 'Big Bertha', was another 'one-off', being built in 1919 for exclusive service on the Lickey incline for banking purposes up the 1 in 37 bank on the Birmingham to Bristol main line some ten miles south of New Street station. It was allocated to Bromsgrove shed and made a fine sight pounding up the Lickey hills. It is seen withdrawn from service at Derby Works on 12th August 1956. (J.D.Gomersall)

71) The former Great North of Scotland Y Class 0-4-2 Tanks first came into service in 1915 with just two examples constructed for use in Aberdeen Docks. They later became the Z5 Class, numbered 68192 and 68193 under British Railways. No 68192 is photographed looking in fine external condition by the turntable of its home shed at 61A Kittybrewster on 26th June 1956. It was taken out of revenue earning service from Kittybrewster in April 1960. (A.N.H.Glover)

72) Freight traffic on the Southern Region of British Railways was rather sparce in comparison with other regions and it was a rare event to 'spot' a Bulleid Pacific at the head of one. SR Unrebuilt *Battle of Britain* Class 4-6-2 No 34058 *Sir Frederick Pile*, from 72A Exmouth Junction, is an exception to the rule as it powers some ballast wagons through Basingstoke station on 6th September 1956. No 34058 was rebuilt at Eastleigh Works in November 1960. (B.K.B.Green)

73) A dull day in Cornwall on 19th August 1956. GWR *County* Class 4-6-0 No 1002 *County of Berks* backs out of Penzance station with its three-coach load which will be shunted into the sidings prior to the locomotive returning to its home shed of 83G. Built in 1945, *County of Berks* was equipped with a double chimney in June 1958. During its latter years of service it was based at 83E St.Blazey, 83D Laira (Plymouth), 81E Didcot and 89A Shrewsbury. (N.L.Browne)

74) Three young lads enjoy the rare 'treat' of a footplate ride at Crewe station, near to the shed at 5A Crewe (North) on 1st September 1956. Their 'host' for a few precious minutes is ex. works BR *Britannia* Class 4-6-2 No 70017 *Arrow*, a visitor to the London Midland Region from 86C Cardiff (Canton). In July 1958 *Arrow* made a permanent move to the LMR after being transferred to 9E Trafford Park where it was based for in excess of two years. (S.Dartnell)

75) In the far off days when the Channel Tunnel was just a dream (or a nightmare!) a lengthy boat train meanders across the still waters of Folkestone Harbour on 9th September 1957, powered by a duet of SR Rl Class 0-6-0 Tanks, Nos 31128 and 31069 which will take the train as far as Folkestone Junction. For a while these services were in charge of GWR 5700 Class 0-6-0 Pannier Tanks. Both Nos 31069 and 31128 had taken their leave of the area by May 1959. (B.K.B.Green)

76) Apart from the main complexes within Glasgow, at 65A Eastfield, 66A Polmadie and 67A Corkerhill, there were a host of other depots both large and small within the metropolis. One such shed was at 65D Dawsholm of former Caledonian Railway origin. Posing alongside the running shed in bright sunlight is Drummond Caledonian Class 2F 0-6-0 No 57336 on 27th August 1957. This engine remained at Dawsholm until May 1962, moving to 67B Hurlford. (N.L.Browne)

77) Begrimed and unwanted it is the end of the road for 86E Severn Tunnel Junction based GWR 3150 Class 2-6-2T No 3150 as it awaits scrapping at Swindon Works on 3rd November 1957 some two months after withdrawal. Built at Swindon in 1906, No 3150 was the oldest unrebuilt 2-6-2T. (Nos 3100/11-49 were in fact built from 1903 onwards, but were rebuilt during 1928-30.) No 3150 lay in store at Swindon Works until cut up in January 1958. (F.Hornby)

78) The world famous *Flying Scotsman* locomotive has been with us for some seventy-two years, forty years in general service and thirty-two years in preservation and is still going strong today, a tribute to the men who built her at Doncaster Works way back in 1923. On a murky summer's day in 1957, No 60103 accelerates out of Peterborough (North) station and emerges from beneath the Crescent bridge with a Cleethorpes to Kings Cross express. (A.C.Ingram)

79) Built in a streamlined form during 1939 at Crewe Works LMS *Coronation* Class 4-6-2 No 46238 *City of Carlisle*, from 12A Carlisle (Upperby), flies through Hest Bank station on the West Coast Main Line with a Glasgow (Central) to Birmingham (New Street) express on 1st September 1957. This locomotive had a lengthy association with Carlisle until rendered redundant by the operating authorities in October 1964. It was scrapped two months later. (R.Butterfield)

80) GWR *King* Class 4-6-0 No 6018 *King Henry VI* stands in the yard of its home shed at 81A Old Oak Common on 10th April 1957 during the occasion of a shed visit by enthusiasts. *King Henry VI* was drafted to 86C Cardiff (Canton) in August 1960, but returned to Old Oak in June 1962. Although officially withdrawn in December 1962 it was retained at 84E Tyseley until the end of April 1963 when it worked a special to Swindon from Birmingham (Snow Hill). (N.L.Browne)

81) One of the least photographed railway workshops was at St.Rollox in Glasgow which turned out locomotives in as fine a condition as its more famous counterparts, as can be seen by an immaculate LNER Bl Class 4-6-0 No 61344, from 65C Parkhead, which is ready to be steamed and returned home on 14th August 1957. This locomotive survived in service until September 1966, from 62A Thornton Junction. It was scrapped at Motherwell in June 1967. (D.K.Jones)

82) The weeds are beginning to take over at the soon to be doomed station at Newick & Chailey as BR Class 4 2-6-4T No 80150, a 75A Brighton steed, pauses briefly with the 12.28pm local passenger from East Grinstead to Lewes on 16th March 1957. Much of this line is now in the capable hands of the Bluebell Railway, but Newick & Chailey station is no longer with us, having closed during 1958. Also with us, thanks to the preservation movement, is No 80150. (F.Hornby)

83) Although of Caledonian Railway origin the shed at 65D Dawsholm also played host to former North British Railways locos after nationalisation. Two examples of the rival companies stand buffer to buffer in the shed yard at 65D on 15th June 1958. Nearest the camera is NBR Y9 Class 0-4-0ST No 68114 (note the primitive buffer) which survived in service until September 1960. Behind is CR Class 3F 0-6-0T No 56238 from 65G Yoker. (N.L.Browne)

84) By the end of 1957 the ranks of the Drummond/Urie/Maunsell inspired SR H15 Class 4-6-0's had been reduced to twenty survivors based at 70A Nine Elms, 71A Eastleigh and 72B Salisbury and the writing was on the wall for them with the class being rendered extinct by December 1961. On 19th April 1958 a member of the footplate crew is busy as his steed, No 30488 (70A), stands in Clapham Junction station with a Windsor lines freight bound for Nine Elms. (N.L.Browne)

85) Under clear signals GWR *Castle* Class 4-6-0 No 5050 *Earl of St.Germans*, paired with a straight -sided tender, powers its way through Wrexham (General) station on a wet and windy 27th September 1958 with an express on the Chester to Shrewsbury main line. Allocated to 84C Shrewsbury, *Earl of St.Germans* went to pastures new at 81A Old Oak Common in September 1960. It was condemned from 82B St.Philip's Marsh in August 1963 after completing 1,135,797 miles. (R.W.Hinton)

86) Following a heavy overhaul at Crewe Works LMS Unrebuilt *Patriot* Class 4-6-0 No 45511 *Isle of Man*, from 1A Willesden, is noted outside the paint shop at Crewe on 23rd February 1958. In October 1959 *Isle of Man* was moved to 24L Carnforth. This was followed by a move to 6B Mold Junction in January 1960 and to 8B Warrington four months later. Its last abode was at 12B Carlisle (Upperby) from whence it was rendered surplus to requirements in February 1961. (N.E.Preedy)

87) The handsome Pickersgill Caledonian Class 3P 4-4-0's (BR Nos 54477-54508) were first introduced during 1920 and a few were destined to survive as late as 1962. In this picture No 54488 is seen on parade alongside its home shed at 60B Aviemore on 19th June 1958. The depot, of Highland Railway pedigree, now belongs to the Strathspey Railway. No 54488 passed into history in February 1961 and was cut up at Inverurie Works two months later. (N.L.Browne)

88) BR *Britannia* Class 4-6-2 No 70002 *Geoffrey Chaucer* emerged into traffic during 1951, being based on the Eastern Region where it was to remain until December 1963 serving from 30A Stratford, 32D Yarmouth South Town, 32A Norwich and 31B March. On 20th April 1958 it is noted at 36A Doncaster still sporting an old 'Lion on Wheel' logo on the tender. Its last years of life were spent at 12A Carlisle (Kingsmoor), being withdrawn in January 1967. (N.E.Preedy)

89) In bright sunshine LNER inspired Peppercorn A1 Class 4-6-2 No 60157 *Great Eastern*, from 34A Kings Cross, threads a path through Nene carriage sidings Peterborough with a down express from Kings Cross in the summer of 1958. *Great Eastern* was one of five examples of the class to be fitted with roller bearings. This modern innovation mattered not when the 'rush to modernise' came into full swing and it was condemned from 36A Doncaster in January 1965. (A.C.Ingram)

90) Under the watchful gaze of four young trainspotters the pioneer GWR *King* Class 4-6-0 No 6000 *King George V*, from 81A Old Oak Common, steams through Weston-Super-Mare station with a westbound express on 20th September 1958. At one time Weston was an extremely popular resort, but has since declined in popularity with the advent of cheap foreign holidays in the sunshine. Although withdrawn in December 1962, *King George V is* still with us today. (N.L.Browne)

91) Fresh from overhaul at the nearby workshops McIntosh Caledonian Class 2P 0-4-4T No 55218 stands next to an unidentified LMS Class 5 4-6-0 in the yard at 65B St.Rollox on 15th June 1958 prior to being steamed and returned to its home base at 63A Perth. Built at St.Rollox works in 1913 as Class 14391 this was probably the last time that No 55218 had a major overhaul with condemnation looming from 63A Perth during January 1960. (F.Hornby)

92) Possibly due to a shortage of motive power SR N Class 2-6-0 No 31810, from 73A Stewarts Lane, is pressed into service at the head of the lengthy 10.45am Herne Hill to Ramsgate holiday extra, which consists of a motley collection of stock. It is seen here arriving at Beckenham Junction on 30th August 1958. Transferred to 73H Dover in May 1959, No 31810 later moved to 71A Eastleigh and 70C Guildford before withdrawal in March 1964. (N.L.Browne)

93) A 'Midland Railway' flavour at Gloucester (Eastgate) station is captured by the camera on a sun-filled 16th June 1958. Midland Railway inspired Class 4F 0-6-0 No 44567, from the nearby shed at 85E Barnwood, stands by the wooden-built signalbox before shunting the stock of a Birmingham (New Street) stopping service via Worcester. Eastgate station is long gone with the site being occupied today by an 'Asda' store. (N.E.Preedy)

94) During 1958 the influx of new diesel locomotives and diesel multiple units began to have an adverse effect on the steam stock on all of the British Railways regions and ranks of condemned engines began to gather in the yards of major workshops prior to disposal. One major dumping ground was at Swindon Works where many locos were stored before being despatched to outside contractors. On 27th July 1958 GWR 4300 Class 2-6-0 No 5397 awaits the call to Woodhams, Barry. (N.L.Browne)

95) Deep in the heart of Cornwall we pause at Camborne station, with its staggered platforms, once of Great Western/West Cornwall Railways, some 292 miles from Paddington. On 14th August 1959 begrimed 83G Penzance GWR *Castle* Class 4-6-0 No 5020 *Trematon Castle* departs from Camborne with a stopping passenger train from Plymouth to Penzance. *Trematon Castle* departed from the West Country for good in September 1961, moving to 88A Cardiff (Canton). (Peter Hay)

96) By 1959 the 'Caley Jumbo's' (LMS Class 2F 0-6-0's) were obviously not going to be around for very much longer, and therefore became proper subjects for photographers capturing the fast changing scene. No 57252 at 63B Stirling shed on 28th March 1959 appears to have been overhauled recently, probably for the last time in its seventy-eight years of life. Even the worksplate, which read 'LMS built 1917 St.Rollox' has had a good polish during the overhaul. (Peter Hay)

97) Barely two years old BR Class 4 2-6-0 No 76102 stands in steam at its home depot at 65B St.Rollox on 20th June 1959 in the company of another St.Rollox locomotive, LMS Class 5 4-6-0 No 45159. Between June 1957 and October 1964, No 76102 remained in the Glasgow area moving around from 65D Dawsholm, 65C Parkhead and 65B St.Rollox. The last two years or so of its life were spent at 65F Grangemouth, 67E Dumfries and 67B Hurlford (Kilmarnock). (A.N.H.Glover)

98) A fine close-up study of one of the magnificent Bulleid Light Pacifics, as photographed in Clapham Junction yard on 11th April 1959. SR *West Country* Class 4-6-2 No 34031 *Torrington*, allocated to 70A Nine Elms, commenced its working life in unrebuilt form in June 1946. In November 1958 it was rebuilt at Eastleigh works and transferred to Nine Elms from 72A Exmouth Junction. The final base for *Torrington* was at 70D Eastleigh, withdrawn in February 1965. (N.L.Browne)

99) A fine array of upper quadrant semaphore signals tower over the West Coast Main Line at Winwick Junction in the summer of 1959. Approaching the camera on quadruped track is Stanier LMS Class 6P5F 2-6-0 No 42950, from 5B Crewe (South), which is charge of a heavy relief express. Ousted from Crewe (South) shed in January 1960, No 42950 worked from a variety of motive power depots until withdrawn from 9F Heaton Mersey in November 1965. (T.Lewis)

100) One of the largest steam depots in South Wales was at Cardiff (Canton) and it was also one of the first to succumb totally to diesel power. In August 1959 steam was still firmly entrenched at 86C as it was then. In a section of the vast yard we espy GWR 5600 Class 0-6-2T No 6621 which is a visitor to the depot from 86H Tondu. Lurking behind No 6621 is a virtually brand new BR Class 9F 2-10-0 No 92222, from 84C Banbury. (N.E.Preedy)

101) Like Cardiff (Canton) in the previous picture, 73C Hither Green also fell victim to the new 'image' and closed to steam early in the sixties, although it retained facilities for visiting locomotives for some years after. In April 1959 SR C Class 0-6-0 No 31682, from 73D Gillingham, stands near the coaling plant at Hither Green a depot it was to serve at from February 1960 until condemnation from the same in October 1961. (N.E.Preedy)

102) Born at Doncaster Works in 1937, LNER A4 Class 4-6-2 No 60008 *Dwight D.Eisenhower* was originally named *Golden Shuttle*. It is seen in splendid fettle at Kings Cross station on 6th July 1959 as it departs with the 3.10pm express to Newcastle. Transferred to 34E New England upon the closure of Kings Cross in June 1963 it was condemned the following month. Today, *Dwight D.Eisenhower* is preserved in the United States of America, a fitting tribute. (M.Joyce)

103) We enter a new decade, the last one as it turned out for steam on British Railways and the end of a way of life. We commence with a look on the bright side and feature an engine in mint condition. After revisiting its birthplace for a major overhaul, GWR *Hall* Class 4-6-0 No 5904 *Kelham Hall*, newly transferred to 82B St.Philip's Marsh from 82D Westbury, stands outside 'A' Shop at Swindon Works, minus tender, in November 1960. (Tim Farebrother)

104) The NER Class E1 0-6-0 Tanks were first introduced by Wilson Worsdell in 1898 and they were continued under Raven in 1914 and 1920's for the LNER by Gresley, strangely built at the GNR works at Doncaster. A further fifteen were constructed by BR in 1950/51 at Darlington Works. No 68738 photographed here at 52B Heaton on 4th September 1960, was originally NER No 2331 built in 1922. These engines were later reclassified as J72. (N.L.Browne)

105) Entering service in December 1934 LMS *Jubilee* Class 4-6-0 No 45639 *Raleigh*, from 55A Leeds (Holbeck), finds itself in the unlikeliest of Western Region outposts at Malvern Wells in the summer of 1960. *Raleigh* must have worked tender-first to Great Malvern on a day excursion before returning northwards to its home base in a more conventional manner. Withdrawn from Holbeck in October 1963, *Raleigh* was scrapped at Crewe Works in January 1964. (Tim Farebrother)

106) Constructed at the nowadays long defunct locomotive works at Brighton in April 1947, SR Rebuilt *Battle of Britain* Class 4-6-2 No 34059 *Sir Archibald Sinclair*, allocated to 72B Salisbury, looks in pristine condition in the shed yard at 71A Eastleigh on 21st March 1960. Not only has *Sir Archibald Sinclair* been overhauled at the nearby workshops, but it has been rebuilt at the same time. It was condemned from Salisbury in May 1966. (F.Hornby)

107) One of twenty-one locomotives designed by Maunsell and introduced in 1928, SR U1 Class 2-6-0 No 31902, from 73J. Tonbridge, rests in the yard at 75A Brighton on Sunday 24th April 1960. The U1 Class was a three-cylinder development of the U Class, of which the prototype, No 31890, was rebuilt from a 2-6-4T originally built in 1925. After a brief spell at 72A Exmouth Junction, No 31902 ended its days of service at 75C Norwood Junction. (Tim Farebrother)

108) Well off the beaten track, Churchward 4700 Class 2-8-0 No 4707 (81C Southall), with steam lifting from its safety valves, moves a lengthy transfer freight eastwards through Salisbury in March 1960. Introduced in April 1923, No 4707 survived until May 1964 being one of the last examples to be withdrawn after a long and useful career hauling fast fitted freights over restricted routes due to its heavy axle loading. (Tim Farebrother)

109) The north-east of England was destined to be one of the last outposts of British Railways steam, which was to be rather ironic as some of the most elderly locomotives still in stock were left to carry the flag long after more modern types had disappeared from the scene. On 21st May 1960 former Great Central Railway 01 Class 2-8-0 No 63755, a local engine, drops off from the rear of a Tyne Dock to Consett train hauled by BR Class 9F 2-10-0 No 92060. (D.K.Jones)

110) Two LMS Class 5 4-6-0's stand outside the paint shop at Crewe Works on 26th June 1960 after being outshopped. Nearest the camera is No 45333, of 15C Leicester (Midland). In the left of the picture are two LMS Unrebuilt *Patriot* Class 4-6-0's, one being in primer. One of them, No 45506 *The Royal Pioneer Corps* is sporting what appears to be a 9A Longsight (Manchester) shedplate, when in fact it was allocated to 82E Bristol Barrow Road on this date. (A.N.H.Glover)

111) By 1961 the writing was on the wall for steam in many parts of East Anglia, including the former Great Eastern Railway outpost at Norwich. In this panoramic view taken on 22nd April 1961, LNER L1 Class 2-6-4T No 67730, from the near-at-hand shed of 32A, leaves a shroud of grey smoke as it passes an English Electric Type 4 Diesel with a parcels train. No 67730 took its leave of Norwich in February 1962, moving to 30A Stratford. (T.R.Amos)

112) 86C Cardiff (Canton) based BR *Britannia* Class 4-6-2 No 70016 *Ariel* shares a dead road with an unidentified GWR *Castle* Class 4-6-0 at 87A Neath on 7th August 1961. The following month *Ariel* was transferred to the London Midland Region and served from no less than seven depots before withdrawal in August 1967 - 12C Carlisle (Canal), 9A Longsight (Manchester), 5A Crewe (North), 6G Llandudno Junction, 6J Holyhead, 21D Aston and 12A Carlisle (Kingmoor). (N.E.Preedy)

113) Newly allocated to 70A Nine Elms from 73B Bricklayers Arms, SR *Schools* Class 4-4-0 No 30935 *Sevenoaks* is flanked by Bulleid Pacifics of both the unrebuilt and rebuilt versions in the depot yard at 70A Nine Elms on a sunny October day in 1961. Once of 73F Ashford, *Sevenoaks* had made the move to Bricklayers Arms in August 1961. It remained at Nine Elms until condemned in December 1962. It was eventually cut up in May 1964 at Kettering. (D.K.Jones)

114) LMS Class 5 4-6-0 No 44945, a longstanding inmate of 21A Saltley, lays a lengthy trail of exhaust smoke as it steams towards the camera at Haresfield on the former Midland main line, between Gloucester and Stonehouse, on 29th July 1961. No 44945 is in charge of a down relief express filled with holidaymakers bound for Bournemouth. This locomotive remained in the Midlands until withdrawn from 2B Oxley in October 1966. (B.W.L.Brooksbank)

133) The robust and versatile LMS Class 3F 'Jinty' 0-6-0 Tanks were a popular choice of motive power as station pilots at the larger stations and Carlisle (Citadel) was no exception. On 28th August 1963, Nos 47288 and 47415, both from 12B Carlisle (Upperby), await their next call to duty on the centre roads at Citadel. No 47288 was condemned from 12B in November 1964, whereas No 47415 survived until July 1966 at 8A Edge Hill (Liverpool) (D.K.Jones)

134) A trio of unkempt locomotives are lined up at the northern end of the running shed at 34E New England on a filthy 1st September 1963. On the left is former 34A Kings Cross inmate LNER A4 Class 4-6-2 No 60021 *Wild Swan* (withdrawn the following month). In the centre is LNER Bl Class 4-6-0 No 61207 (withdrawn in December 1963 from 34E). On the right is a visitor from 18A Toton, LMS Class 8F 2-8-0 No 48149, condemned from 8G Sutton Oak in January 1967. (K.L.Seal)

135) Allocated for many years at 81B Slough, GWR 5700 Class 0-6-0PT No 4650 was drafted to South Wales in May 1960, initially to 87D Swansea East Dock. In July 1961 it was on the move again, this time to 86F Aberbeeg where it is seen in the shed yard on 1st June 1963. For trainspotters travelling by train the shed was a quarter of an hour's walk from Aberbeeg station, that is until 1962 when it was closed to passengers. The shed closed in 1964. (N.E.Preedy)

136) A 'stranger in the camp' at St.Pancras station on 11th May 1963. Enthusiasts wait in crocodile formation to 'cab' SR Unrebuilt *West Country* Class 4-6-2 No 34006 *Bude*, from 70A Nine Elms, which is in charge of a joint LCGB/RCTS railtour. After many years of service at Nine Elms, *Bude* was despatched westwards to 70E Salisbury in September 1964 where it remained until condemned in March 1967. It was cut up by Cashmores, Newport. (D.K.Jones)

137) A selection of garden sheds/garages, coaching stock and wagons fill the background at Perth station on a wet and dismal looking 11th August 1963 as LNER A4 Class 4-6-2 No 60027 *Merlin*, allocated to 65B St.Rollox, steams past with a Dundee line express. Once a longstanding resident of 64B Haymarket, *Merlin* had been at St.Rollox shed since May 1962. It ended its days of revenue earning service in September 1965 from 64A St.Margarets. (D.K.Jones)

138) A splendid internal view of a running shed as it was in the days of steam with several different locomotive types on view at 8F Springs Branch Wigan. Nearest the camera is Riddles War Department Austerity Class 8F 2-8-0 No 90464, from 8G Sutton Oak, which is minus some coupling rods on 23rd March 1963. Until September 1960, No 90464 had been based at Carlisle (Kingmoor) depot. It survived in service until March 1964 and was scrapped at Crewe Works. (D.K.Jones)

139) The NODEK (no decay) sign in the background advertising reinforced concrete in William Way's (the builders merchants) yard at Wimbledon was a feature near to the station for many years. It is visible here behind begrimed BR Class 4 4-6-0 No 75077 (70A Nine Elms) on 26th June 1964. No 75077, equipped with a double chimney in June 1961, had been an inmate of 70D Basingstoke for many years. Its last days were spent at Eastleigh shed. (A.F.Nisbet)

140) Until depots began to close by the score a host of steam engines remained on the books of a single depot for years and years. Such was the case with former Great Central Railway 04/8 Class 2-8-0 No 63706 seen in a disgraceful external condition in the shed yard at Staveley G.C., coded 38D and 41H in BR days, on 1st February 1964. Upon the closure of the shed in June 1965, No 63706 went to 41J Langwith Junction, but the stay was shortlived. (Geoff Readman)

141) Mounds of discarded ash from the smokeboxes and grates of countless steam engines present a hazard in the shed yard at 70A Nine Elms in May 1964 where the pioneer SR *Merchant Navy* Class 4-6-2 No 35001 *Channel Packet*, a local engine, is on duty with other Bulleid Pacifics. Constructed In February 1941, *Channel Packet* was rebuilt at Eastleigh Works in August 1959. Transferred to 70F Bournemouth in September 1964 it was withdrawn two months later. (A.C.Ingram)

142) A group of schoolboy spotters are huddled together on a platform at Swindon station on 28th March 1964 as GWR inspired but BR built *Castle* Class 4-6-0 No 7032 *Denbigh Castle*, flanked by two lower quadrant signals, pauses to take refreshment whilst in charge of down milk empties. This was another locomotive which was loyal to one depot for many years - 81A Old Oak Common, from which *Denbigh Castle* was condemned from in September 1964. (F.Hornby)

143) The semi-derelict Holgate excursion platforms provided an ideal 'bolt-hole' for enthusiasts and spotters alike who wished to avoid possible eviction from the station at York in the distance. On 19th May 1964, 50A York based LNER A1 Class 4-6-2 No 60150 *Willbrook* has been relegated to the minor duty of shunting stock, a far cry from the work it was designed to do. Once of 52A Gateshead, No 60150 survived at 50A until October 1964. (H.L.Holland)

144) The massive thirty-two road, half-covered roundhouse at Carlisle (Upperby), coded 12A and 12B by BR, was a good twenty minute's walk from Citadel station but well worth the effort before steam declined. For many years it housed members of the mighty LMS *Coronation* Class 4-6-2's until their extinction in October 1964. One example, No 46250 *City of Lichfield*, poses in the depot yard near to the roundhouse on 30th March 1964. (N.E.Preedy)

145) Although a small number of GWR *Castle* Class 4-6-0's managed to soldier on into 1965, 1964 was really the last year when they were around in significant numbers. On 9th August 1964 a duet of them, Nos 7025 *Sudeley Castle* (85A Worcester) and 7029 *Clun Castle*, a local steed, are noted together near to the coaling stage at 81A Old Oak Common in company with GWR 9400 Class 0-6-0PT No 8498 (81A). The shed closed to steam traction in March 1965. (C.P.Stacey)

146) 1964 was also the last year for main line steam workings to and from Exeter (Central) to Waterloo and as a subsequence Exmouth Junction shed lost its allocation of Bulleid Pacifics by the autumn of that year. Taken over by the Western Region authorities in September 1963, Exmouth Junction had changed codes from 72A to 83D. On 2nd August 1964, just one month away from withdrawal, SR Unrebuilt *Battle of Britain* Class 4-6-2 No 34078 *222 Squadron* is noted at St.Davids station. (D.Webster)

147) A line-up of locomotives near to the coaling plant at 65A Eastfield (Glasgow) in August 1965. Nearest the camera is LNER B1 Class 4-6-0 No 61347, a visitor to 65A from 64C Dalry Road in Edinburgh. Constructed at Gorton Works in May 1949, No 61347 was destined to be one of the last surviving steam engines in Scotland, being withdrawn from 62A Thornton Junction in April 1967. In the left of the frame is BR Class 4 2-6-4T No 80113. (N.E.Preedy)

148) By the summer of 1965 the London Midland authorities were firmly entrenched in the former Western Region in the Midlands. Even the old Western lower quadrant signals had been replaced in many areas by LMR style upper quadrants, like the ones seen here at Tyseley station. LMS Class 5 4-6-0 No 45042 (6B Mold Junction) heads south with a mixed freight. Built at the Vulcan Foundry in October 1934, No 45042 survived until September 1967. (Tim Farebrother)

149) Bright sunshine and deep shadows at Ryde Pier Head station on 18th April 1965 as the Isle of Wight prepares itself for the forthcoming summer season with holidaymakers and all the fun of the fair. A 'steamer' lurks in the background as SR 02 Class 0-4-0T No 22 *Brading*, with a partially scorched smokebox, prepares to depart with the 2.25pm local passenger train to Ventnor. Like many sister engines *Brading* was withdrawn in December 1966. (J.Schatz)

150) A rarely photographed shed was at Lower Darwen, which was not surprising as it was a forty five minute walk from Blackburn station if on foot. Constructed by the Lancashire and Yorkshire Railway it carried the codes of 24D and 10H until complete closure on 14th February 1966. Photographed on the turntable at the depot on 13th March 1965 is WD Class 8F 2-8-0 No 90556, a local inhabitant which was condemned from 10H during this same month. (R.G.B.Jackson)

151) It is the eleventh hour for steam at 81C Southall on 18th February 1965 with closure on the horizon. In the foreground of this picture are two GWR 6100 Class 2-6-2 Tanks, Nos 6106 (81C) and 6159 a visitor to Southall from 81E Didcot. Hemmed between these two locomotives is another visitor in the shape of LMS Class 8F 2-8-0 No 48120, from 2B Oxley. After withdrawal in December 1965, No 6106 was saved by the preservation movement. (M.S.Stokes)

152) Sporting express passenger headcode lamps, LMS Class 4 2-6-4T No 42152, of 56A Wakefield, rattles towards the camera at Wrenthorpe with the 17.00hrs Bradford to Kings Cross train which it is working tender-first as far as Leeds on 17th June 1965. From January 1957 until condemnation in October 1967, No 42152 worked from 56D Mirfield, 56A Wakefield (twice), 55F Manningham, 55A Leeds (Holbeck) and 56F Low Moor sheds. (D.K.Jones)

153) Constructed by British Railways in September 1949, SR *West Country* Class 4-6-2 No 34093 *Saunton* was rebuilt at Eastleigh in May 1960. It spent much of its working life on the former London and South Western Main Line between Waterloo and Weymouth being allocated to the sheds at 71B Bournemouth, 70A Nine Elms and 70D Eastleigh. On 26th June 1965 it is noted near to the Motive Power depot at Basingstoke as a light engine. (N.E.Preedy)

154) Ousted by diesel traction from its old haunts from Liverpool Street to Norwich, BR *Britannia* Class 4-6-2 No 70041 *Sir John Moore* found itself at 40B Imingham by December 1960 and it remained there for three years, often employed on the fish trains from Grimsby over the former Great Central Main Line. By December 1963 it was drafted to the Carlisle area. On 3rd June 1965 it is seen minus nameplates outside 66E Carstairs shed. (N.E.Preedy)

155) With the potential fire hazard of a timber yard near at hand, former North Eastern Railway Q6 Class 0-8-0 No 63450, its paintwork burnt and peeling, leaks steam as it wheezes out of West Hartlepool station with a pick-up freight on 16th June 1966. Once of 50C Selby, No 63450 moved to the new shed at 51L Thornaby in June 1959, thence to 51C West Hartlepool three years later. It was taken out of revenue earning service in December 1966 from 51C. (N.E.Preedy)

156) Pacific power at rest in the shed yard at 70D Eastleigh on 5th June 1966. Nearest the camera is SR Unrebuilt *Battle of Britain* Class 4-6-2 No 34066 *Spitfire*, of 70E Salisbury. Behind *Spitfire* is SR Rebuilt *Battle of Britain* Class 4-6-2 No 34059 *Sir Archibald Sinclair* which by coincidence is also a Salisbury steed. Both locomotives were condemned during 1966. In the right of the frame is Birmingham Railway Carriage & Wagon Type 3 Diesel No D6585. (D.Titheridge)

157) A panoramic view of the interior of the straight running shed at 8F Springs Branch Wigan on 27th July 1966 where several locomotive types are on view including representatives of BR and LMS classes. In the left of the picture is BR Class 4 2-6-0 No 76077 which is a visitor to Springs Branch from 8G Sutton Oak. As the sixties progressed the allocation at 8F diminished and during 1967/68 it was used as a dumping ground for condemned engines. (C.P.Stacey)

158) For countless years there was a shed at the remote outpost of Tebay which provided banking engines up the formidable Shap incline but by May 1966 most of the work for these engines was confined to assisting freight trains as can be seen in this photograph of LMS Class 4 2-6-4T No 42154 as it lends a hand with a northbound freight at Greenholme. No 42154 was withdrawn from traffic in January 1967 and scrapped at Campbells, Airdrie. (N.E.Preedy)

159) A splendid close-up profile of the final member of the SR *Merchant Navy* Class 4-6-2's, No 35030 *Elder Dempster Lines*, from 70G Weymouth, as it waits at Brockenhurst station with an express on 9th May 1966. *Elder Dempster Lines* was turned out by British Railways in April 1949 and rebuilt just nine years later. Most of its working life was spent at 70A Nine Elms and indeed it was withdrawn from there in July 1967 at the end of Southern steam. (B.K.B.Green)

160) One can almost smell the atmosphere inside the cathedral like roundhouses at 50A York on 24th June 1966. At rest near to the turntable is former NER J27 Class 0-6-0 No 65823, a local inhabitant of 50A, which went on to work at 52F Blyth and 52G Sunderland before being rendered redundant in March 1967. Next to No 65823 is BR Class 9F 2-10-0 No 92172, from 36A Doncaster. Though in steam, No 92172 was condemned a few days later. (M.Turner)

161) Although involved heavily in the construction of diesel locomotives, on 9th January 1966 a section of the vast workshops at Crewe still carried out major overhauls of steam engines. Focus of this print is 12A Carlisle (Kingmoor) BR *Britannia* Class 4-6-2 No 70040 *Clive of India* which is undergoing what is possibly its last major repairs before withdrawal in April 1967. In front of No 70040 is a frame from BR Class 9F 2-10-0 No 92107. (D.Titheridge)

162) With only four days of life left on the former Great Central Main Line, LMS Class 5 4-6-0 No 44858, from 16B Colwick, pauses at Harrow with the 8.15am express from Nottingham (Victoria) to Marylebone, consisting of just four coaches. After these services ceased, No 44858 was transferred to 8L Aintree where it remained until August 1967. A final transfer took it to 12A Carlisle (Kingmoor) where it died in December 1967. (W.G.Piggott)

163) Stripped of name, number and shedplates 70A Nine Elms based SR Rebuilt *West Country* Class 4-6-2 No 34001 *Plymouth* stands steamless within the interior of 70F Bournemouth on 1st July 1967, a few short days before the end of steam on the Southern Region. Once of 73B Bricklayers Arms and 73A Stewarts Lane, *Plymouth* had also been at Nine Elms between May 1961 and September 1964. It was withdrawn from service a few days after this photo was taken. (J.M.Gascoyne)

164) The once common sight of an engine and brake was fading fast on the British Railways scene when this photograph of former North Eastern Railway J27 Class 0-6-0 No 65892 was taken on 12th June 1967. No 65892 (52G Sunderland) steams beneath a signal gantry at Ryehope Junction, Sunderland and heads for its next designated task. Condemned in August 1967 it was stored briefly before being despatched to Willoughbys, Choppington for scrapping. (N.E.Preedy)

165) Another locomotive which survived to the bitter end on the Southern was BR Class 5 4-6-0 No 73065, from 70A Nine Elms, seen here in the carriage sidings on the Windsor lines at Clapham Junction in the spring of 1967. In its earlier days of life No 73065 was based at Millhouses and Canklow on the London Midland/Eastern Regions. It was drafted to the Southern in December 1962 and worked at a variety of sheds before condemnation. (Peter Hay)

166) Two months away from withdrawal, begrimed BR Class 9F 2-10-0 No 92050 is steamed and ready for its next duty in the shed yard at 8C Speke Junction, its home depot on 18th July 1967. From January 1957, No 92050 was allocated to 18A Toton (twice), Rugby Testing Station, 21A Saltley, 17C Rowsley, 16E Kirkby-in-Ashfield and 9D Newton Heath. In February 1966 it arrived at Speke Junction. Its final base (briefly) was at 8B Warrington. (N.E.Preedy)